Forgive Me

NAVIGATING LIFE AFTER SURVIVAL MODE

TAKHIA GAITHER

I Forgive Me

Navigating Life After Survival Mode

TAKHIA GAITHER

The Ready Write-Her

Disclaimer: This book should not replace or supersede any information you have received from a licensed medical professional. Please adhere to the advice and guidance of your physicians and ask them any questions you may have about the material presented here should they arise.

ISBN: 979-8-9881944-0-8 (Paperback)
ISBN: 979-8-9881944-1-5 (Ebook)

Library of Congress Control Number: 2023907667

All scripture quotations are taken from the Holy Bible, New International Version®, NIV® Copyright ©1973, 1978, 1984, 2011 by Biblica, Inc.® Used by permission. All rights reserved worldwide.

Front cover image by The Ready Write-Her
Book design by The Ready Write-Her

Printed in the United States of America.

First printing edition 2023.

The Ready Write-Her
Takhia Gaither
Subject: Attention – Permissions Requested/Bulk Orders
thereadywrite-her@tsgsgroup.com/takhia@tsgsgroup.com
thereadywrite-her.com

DEDICATION

To everyone who's ever felt the sting, pain, and discomfort of living life in survival mode, I hold space for you.

ACKNOWLEDGMENTS

- Without God's grace, mercy, and guidance, I would not be here to share this information with you. I WILL bless the Lord at all times and His praises will always be in my mouth! Thank You Jesus!

- To my sons, bonus babies, and the rest of the Gaither/Washington/Baker party of 20 that always shows up, I don't ever have enough words. I love all y'all all the time. Without any of you, I wouldn't be me. Watching all of you go through things reminded me of who I am and how I live.

- To my family and fri-mily, (friends that became/are family), I love you all and thank you for your continued love and support.

- To Lady Norma & my Chosen Pen family and Dr. LaTracey McDougal & the Black Authors Rock family thank you for all the lessons, chats, how-to conversations, and for your yesses that have helped me fulfill mine

- To everyone, everywhere, all the time, THANK YOU!!

TABLE OF CONTENTS

How to Best Use this Book

Transparent moment, my initial thought was to do like most people and just write my story, with some reflective points along the way and let the reader do with the information whatever they decided they needed to do with it. God always pre-empts, hi-jacks, and alters my plans for His and so it turned into a reflective workbook with action item activities for you to work through and on your own healing.

This book is not meant to be read all at one time. There is no day count for completion, however, I would recommend taking on a chapter per week or if you're feeling up to it per day. There's a lot to unpack, literally and figuratively, within these pages.

As always, if you begin to feel overwhelmed, it's ok to take a break and come back to it. You should try to persevere past your initial angst and not give up at the first sight of a challenge. But do listen to yourself and trust your feelings. Some topics will feel heavy but as you work through them, you should feel the heaviness lift. If you are having a hard time, please contact someone to help you – a trusted friend/confidant, a coach, or a medical professional.

You'll want to have something to write with, your Bible, (or device for the Bible App), colored pens, highlighters, and perhaps extra paper or a journal. There is writing space within the chapters and there are blank pages throughout and at the end of the book to help you keep all your thoughts in one place to refer to later.

Before we start, join me in prayer.

Father God,

We come to You this day to thank You for life. We thank You for our experiences and thank You for just being God. We thank You for the love You have shown toward us. As we go through these activities, please touch the heart and mind of the reader. Open their ears, hearts, and eyes to be able to hear, feel, and see all that You need them to as they journey in forgiving themselves and begin/continue to do the work of healing from the traumatic events that were sent to rob us of our Divine Purposes and callings. Thank You for always walking with us and we pray that You never leave our sides. Please be our peace and comfort when they are needed. And Lord, just as You provided safe spaces for me on my journey, please do the same for the reader of these pages. We give You thanks, praise, honor, and glory for all things.

In Jesus' name, we pray, Amen

Introduction

Laundry. It never ever seems to be done. Wash, fold or not fold, put away, leave it out, it's just always there. Yet, lately, it's been the task that gets my creative juices flowing. I fold clothes and I get to thinking. Realistically, any type of cleaning chore puts me in that head space now. Could be low-key therapeutic. Could be because it's the one time that there's nothing else going on. Even if I happen to have some movie or streaming show in the background, my mind just wanders, and I finally get a chance to think about all the things that I've been actively trying not to think about. You know what I mean?

Oddly enough, cleaning used to be the only time that I got to be alone to think. For a number of years, the only peace I could seem to get, even in my own house, was to be in the basement doing laundry. Life was much different back then. Maybe you can relate to some of this. The house always seemed to just have people in it, especially on the weekends. Not just the actual residents of the home, but other people, and they'd be there, comfortable, and everywhere! I didn't have an eat-in kitchen so outside of cooking, I couldn't sit in there. The kids' room was theirs. Even when I tried to sit in my room someone would come in to disturb me, regardless of what I was doing. Or it'd already be occupied so I couldn't find any peace there. The living room and dining room had a bunch of people in them. But the basement was unfinished and not particularly comfortable. There was no furniture except one of those cook-out chairs. You know the ones that come with the bag and flip out and have a cup holder on at least one side.

I used to think it was normal. Par for the course of having a blended family and children of my own. You just go with whatever was going on and it was ok if you didn't have a minute for yourself because it was only the weekend and if all else failed, there was always the peace of the 15-minute ride to work on Monday morning. Now that life doesn't look anything like that, I realize how abnormal it actually was. It was downright exhausting. My very own version of the Twilight Zone except I didn't have the luxury of a narrator to tell me I was in it. But it wasn't the Twilight Zone, in my opinion, it was someplace far worse … Survival Mode.

Survival Mode is that place where you are living a fake normal life and you just do what you need to get by. Your only goal is to survive to see the next day. In my case, I wanted to survive the weekend to see work on Monday, which came with its own things, but it was still peaceful to me.

Can you believe that I found "peace" dealing with other people's children for 7 hours a day even though I couldn't tolerate being in a house full of people all weekend? Crazy right? It was, but what made work more peaceful was the planning periods! I could sit, usually uninterrupted, twice a day for at least 45 whole minutes! I did not have to talk or interact with anyone if I didn't feel like it. I enjoyed hall duty because I picked the most obscure spot, with hardly any traffic, and I could just chill out and listen to the choir kids or the band or whoever was practicing for the upcoming show. But I digress …

Sounds fun right? I hope you caught the sarcasm. Or maybe you didn't because you just now realized that you've been in your own Survival Mode and those two 45-minute breaks sound like heaven. Either way, I get it. My new favorite saying for things is "I overstand." I've done all the under I can do. There's nothing left to understand, we passed that a long time ago. I'm also over it all. So, I overstand only makes sense. Most people get it.

In talking to my counselor about writing this book and some other topics, she asked how long I thought I was in Survival Mode. My best guess was at least 8 years because I began to notice it more after my oldest child was born. When I really stopped to think about it, I'd probably been there much longer because everything started before he was even born. The difference was that before becoming a mother, I lived alone so it was easier to dial out of it all once everyone left, but it still very much existed.

Thank God for the pandemic. I know some people feel differently and I hope I haven't offended anyone, but for me, the shutdowns and everything else saved my life. Those years are what brought me out of Survival Mode and opened my eyes to the fact that it had been exhausting living the way I was living.

Whether you're wondering if you're in it, just realizing you are, have started to come out, or have been out of Survival Mode for quite some time, there will be something in this book for you. Coming out requires intentional thoughts and actions. It doesn't happen overnight. But I will say that realizing you're no longer in that space can happen out of nowhere, (at least it did for me, but we'll talk about that later). One of the major keys of it all is forgiveness. Without it, you will stay spinning, which is almost as bad as Survival Mode itself.

Per my usual disclaimer, grab your pen, highlighter, and Bible, and let's go to work!

CHAPTER 1
Survival Mode Defined

The Jefferson Center, a nonprofit community-focused mental health care and substance use provider defines survival mode as your brain booting in "safe mode" due to some sort of trauma, prolonged grief, or burnout. Trauma doesn't necessarily mean physical injury and grief may not necessarily be associated with the death of a person. For instance, if you grew up with a drug-addicted parent, you may have been subjected to childhood trauma and began to do things to operate within the circumstances you were living in. Or you could be grieving a divorce in which you feel you were blindsided. Think of it this way, survival mode is like that blue screen popping up on your computer to tell you something is wrong, and it needs to start in safe mode to not cause further damage to your device.

Our brains are really cool. The more I study about the body period, the more amazed I become. It's a bit of a "Wow God!" moment as I learn all the things that our bodies and especially brains can do to keep us safe and well. Your brain has four responses to any traumatic type of event - fight, flight, freeze, and fawn. These are natural and it is normal for them to happen in response to those situations. What's not normal is when one becomes dominant and that's kind of where you stay or when you stay in that mode even where there's no trauma present. I'll explain each of these in a little more detail.

Fight - When you face everything head-on as if it's a major confrontation. An example of this is when someone is quick to fight all the time. You can ask the simplest of questions and they are on 100, looking for boxing gloves to go rounds in the ring.

Flight - When you do everything possible to avoid a confrontation. It may mean literally running away. It might be hiding. It might be avoiding things. Whether we realize it or not, social media provides a way to be in flight regularly. To escape the reality of our own lives, we will sit and scroll endlessly looking at other people's.

Freeze – This happens when you do absolutely nothing. You feel powerless, hopeless, and like there is nothing that can be done to make it any better or to change anything. I think of this one as the deer in the headlights crossed with Eeyore. You stand still watching everything come towards you all while saying "Oh well it's not going to change anyway," so you sit, sulk, and don't take any action at all.

Fawn - When you try to come up with something to make the situation less threatening or non-threatening at all. This one is where people-pleasers live. They try their best to make everything agreeable, even if it contradicts their own beliefs and values.

As I've said, all of these are natural. Every once in a while, you will hear something that sets you into a mode where you feel the need to fight. In a state of shock, you may either be in flight mode and leave if that's possible or freeze because it's not. Sometimes, you may find yourself doing something that will definitely please someone else although you don't necessarily want to. The problem is that we either stay in whatever state too long or they're just all on heavy rotation all the time, which makes you hypervigilant about everything. In classes I've taken, they say that one of these is always your main go-to but when you can rationalize a situation, you can process and determine a better or different reaction. When you're in survival mode, there's a dominant one and then a secondary one. For me, the fight was dominant. You were not going to say or do anything to me without me calling you out on it and if it came to a literal fight, then so be it, we could square up now and get to scrappin'. To be honest, my fight is still dominant. Thanks be to God that I've learned to use it properly and not be antagonized by everything. My second was flight. I was never interested in people pleasing and I'm generally a quick thinker so freezing wasn't it. I would happily avoid, especially things I didn't deem worth the fight.

Here is where it's time to do some work. Take a moment to really think about what your top two responses are. If you feel like you need to, jot down specific examples of each. If you can't narrow it down to two of them, it's ok. The important thing is to take some time to realize what these things look like for you. I'm going to paraphrase, and show my age at the same time, using a saying from G. I. Joe cartoons from the '80s. "You need to know and knowing is half the battle." Once you know what your reactions are, you can begin to think about the events that trigger these reactions, (we'll talk more about triggers in the next chapter). Remember, if any of

the topics or exercises start to feel heavy or be too much, take

a break from reading and/or doing them. Feel free to complete

them with the help of a counselor, therapist, or coach. I have

included a few blank pages here for you to jot down notes, if

you need more space, use a journal or additional sheets of

paper.

Reflection: *What is your primary survival response? If you can't identify it right away, think about situations you've been in and jot down notes about the event and your response to it.*

_____

_____

_____

_____

_____

_____

_____

_____

_____

_____

_____

_____

_____

_____

_____

_____

_____

_____

_____

_____

_____

_____

_____

_____

_____

_____

_____

_____

_____

_____

_____

_____

_____

_____

_____

CHAPTER 2
Triggers ... They Do Come

There was a commercial on TV when I was growing up for an adult beverage and the tagline was "Don't let the smooth taste fool you." Most of the time that is exactly how I feel every time I sit down to write. Oh, I can put some words together like nobody's business. God shows off when the pen's up! The outcome is a surprise for me as well. Even with that, there's always that little annoying voice that tries to whisper, "You ain't even healed, how you goin' to tell anybody else anything?" But that's the thing. I suffered in silence for a number of years. I will heal out loud and scream it from the mountaintops if I have to. That's the gift of the teacher. Everything's a lesson. And writing is therapeutic.

What does any of that have to do with triggers? I got you, just follow along. A very popular streaming show premiered right before the holidays in 2022. I purposely did not watch it. One because I couldn't be torn away from Hallmark, Lifetime, Aspire, and UP TV long enough to watch anything other than the Christmas movie lineup. More than that, prior to being turned into a streaming show, the program was a two-part movie. The first part was very entertaining, the second part was kind of heavy. I wasn't sure what to expect from the new thing and after seeing mixed reviews across social media, I left it on the "watch later" list.

Starting in January of this year, (2023), I declared the weekend as my self-care time. No writing or editing for anyone else unless I just really wanted to. With that came my relaxation of binge-watching whatever since I don't generally watch TV during the week. I watched the whole series in less than 24 hours and by the time it got to the end, I was beyond grateful that I did not jump on the viewing bandwagon in December. Not because it was a poor show but because from start to finish, it would have been an extremely emotional rollercoaster at a time when I was coming to grips with some pretty big realities.

There were two big keys for me coming out of survival mode, 1 - Listening to God and 2 - Trusting the still small calming voice within. In the past, I did not do either of those things very well because I was convinced I was paranoid or overthinking things. In the case of this particular show, doing those things showed me the difference that listening and waiting made. Two months ago, I wouldn't have been able to sit down and pin a book a chapter after viewing the show. I would have been stuck in my feelings and in my head and realistically, probably would have made myself sick to my stomach. All stories, even the ones that are fiction, at some point have probably been someone else's reality. Watching anything that has to do with infidelity, divorce, or anything that remotely mirrors abuse is still very much a trigger for me.

However, because I am aware that they are, very rarely have they been fired because I've learned to recognize them, have my feelings, and let them go. It sounds really simple, right? Now it is, but in the beginning, it wasn't. You have to give yourself grace through recovery. Whatever situation caused you to go into survival mode, didn't happen overnight. Healing and recovery will not either. It will get better day by day.

Exercise number two. This one cannot be done in one sitting. It's usually situational. Now that you're aware of what your top responses are and what it looks like for you to respond in that way, start paying close attention to situations, activities, and interactions that put you into that frame of mind. For example, you know how Facebook shows you the memories of your past posts? Seeing those memories usually made me want to try again whenever I'd deemed a specific relationship was over. When things officially ended, I no longer felt nostalgic, but I began to grow extremely angry which sent me into fight mode, over anything! I would be in that frame of mind from the time I saw that memory until well into the next day. To alleviate these prolonged angry events, I began to delete the photo memories therefore not firing the trigger. It doesn't mean that I've ignored the photos or even my own thoughts when they arise but I can healthily process those memories without walking around angry all day.

Now it's your turn. You may choose to write them down or just keep a mental note. Spend some time paying attention to what triggers you. As a writer, I suggest writing everything down. Not to keep things memorialized but because writing opens up your mind and has great benefits. Open-mindedness helps when processing your thoughts, responses, and triggers. As you begin to see things as they are, it will help you to make different and healthier choices in dealing with those situations. Another benefit is that you tend to remember things you've had to write down. One of the ways that we stay in prolonged survival mode is that we don't remember how situations affect us. Even if we've seen them play out time and time again with the same or similar ending, we convince ourselves that the next time will be different, but we don't change anything about our behavior to make the difference. Writing it, and then going back to read it, gives you a visual of the pattern so that you can begin to break it.

Lastly, these are not easy topics to face alone. In fact, you shouldn't deal with them alone. I'm sure I've said it already, but just in case, please enlist the help of a licensed counselor, therapist, or trauma-informed coach. Your friends and family love you but often they are not ready to face the realities of your situation. Unless your church has a specific mental health ministry, liaison, or program, many of our church leaders are not prepared to provide the counsel needed for these situations. The primary concern of pastors and ministry leads is the care of your soul. Although many will provide a listening ear and in some way offer assistance, when dealing with these situations, it can be the equivalent of talking to friends and family. You should, however, go to them to cover you in prayer and for any questions that you may have about strengthening, renewing, or starting your walk with Christ.

Reflection: *What triggers you? And how have you dealt with it in the past? Has that method been beneficial, or would you benefit from finding a new way? What could the new way consist of?*

_____

_____

_____

_____

_____

_____

_____

_____

_____

_____

_____

_____

_____

_____

_____

_____

CHAPTER 3
The Great Reset

I remind you, survival mode was never meant to be a permanent head space. It should only be visited when necessary. The deceptive part of it all is that in most cases you won't or didn't even know you were in survival mode until you weren't. For some, it takes intervention from a counselor or trusted voice to point it out, for others you just kind of "wake up." As various things began to unravel for me, I would listen to Katy Perry's "Wide Awake" on repeat. The situation that led me to survival mode was an emotionally abusive relationship. I would fight to hold on to it, or just decide that whatever incident was currently happening, I wasn't going to deal with it. We separated in September 2020 and were divorced in July 2022, yet I didn't fully realize I was out of survival mode, until September 2022.

Resets happen in different ways and spaces but one thing that appears to be common is that there is a level of healthy self-reflection involved. I specifically say healthy because when you are in survival mode, you will also self-reflect but your decisions are still clouded by the trauma that you feel or may actually be facing. One morning while working, I was having a talk with Jesus because that's what I do to help me get things done. I began thinking about various actions I'd recently taken that made sense but didn't all at the same time. Have you ever done that? Thought about something and wondered why that was the choice you made and what led you to that? I'm analytical and logical, these thoughts are always occurring. Usually, I have some sort of answer for why I chose A over B. On this specific day, I did not and more than that, I couldn't think of one either. I asked, "Lord, why in the world did I pick that?" He answered back, "Because you're still thinking from a place you no longer live." Insert the little emoji with the top of the head blown off for your mind being blown because that was me at that moment.

I had to sit with that a bit. It wasn't an easy pill to swallow but it was necessary. One of my ongoing prayers, especially in the last 5-7 years of my life has been "Lord, show me, me. What is my part in all of this?" Although the reason we end up in survival mode is due to our thoughts, feelings, emotions, and responses to the actions of another, the reality is that we all had a part to play. This is not the beat-yourself-up conversation or the one where you begin to take the blame for how people treated you and what they did to you. Nor do you blame yourself for the choices you made. You own them and say yes, I made them. And this is where our forgiveness journey begins.

Coming out of toxic and abusive relationships is hard. Throughout the duration of that event, at more than one time, you've taken the blame and shouldered the responsibility for whatever has taken place. Not necessarily because you wanted to, but because you thought doing so would change the situation for the better. You took on the onus of being the one to change, compromise, and be a better person to a person that really had no thought to be better toward you. That last one stung a bit, huh? Listen, I get it, it still stings for me too! Take some deep breaths and pause if you need to, when you're ready, we're going to get into this reset.

In Acts 27, the Apostle Paul recounts his departure from Rome and the storm that ensued. Although he warned the captain not to continue on, his warning was not heeded, and the boat went head-on into the storm. They were in the midst of heavy rains, had to throw over cargo, and finally had to abandon ship at the risk of prisoners on the boat escaping and/or lives being lost to drowning. However, not one of the men was lost and they all made it to dry land safely, bruised and battered but otherwise safe. I'm going to give you some space here before we move on to read the story in its entirety and jot down what the Lord is saying to you from it. Don't read ahead yet. Let God's word bring you comfort, encouragement, and inspiration. Before we break, let's pray.

Father in the name of Jesus,

We come to You to thank You for this time. I thank You for the reader, their lives, and for their stories. I thank You Lord that You have spared us from our storms and although we may be bruised and battered, we are now in a place to be otherwise safe. As they read, let Your word speak to them in a special way. Open their eyes, ears, and hearts to receive Your comfort, love, and guidance. I pray for and over them as they battle with these tough situations and thoughts. And Lord just like the Apostle Paul, I stand in the gap for them to declare, that not one life will be lost but all will begin to move and continue to walk in Your designed purpose for them.

In Jesus' name, we pray, Amen.

Reflection: *Write down your thoughts as you read Acts 27.*

_____

_____

_____

_____

_____

_____

_____

_____

_____

_____

_____

_____

_____

_____

_____

_____

_____

Now that you've read and gathered your own thoughts, I'll share mine. I'm going to list them here and dedicate a chapter to each to go into detail.

1. It's ok to be there.

2. Pray it through.

3. Movement may not mean you're out.

4. Don't be afraid to throw away things.

5. LIVE!

6. Believe that you are the overcomer.

7. Assess the damages and move on.

CHAPTER 4
It's OK to be Here

A s I typed out the title of the chapter, so many things flooded me at once. For starters it is ok for you to be HERE, literally, on Earth, breathing, living, moving, and being. You are allowed to be. It is also OK for you to be HERE as in the place of survival mode. Remember back to the beginning, survival mode is created by your brain, which means God made it. It was the mechanism He put within us to protect and shield ourselves from harmful situations until we can process them. The problem is that when we're faced with repeated trauma, we never get to switch off. At some point, we are supposed to be able to turn it off.

I know a lot of this may seem repetitive and I can admit, it is and it will be. That's for multiple reasons. Reason #1 - Repetition is one of the keys to teaching. Most people don't just learn from a one-and-done type of lesson. It requires sessions of repetition and practice to be able to fully grasp and understand what is being taught. Even those who pick up things quickly, still need the repetition to commit the processes to memory. Reason #2 - It's been a compound event. Each thing builds on the other, or really since we're kind of going in reverse, it may be better to think in terms of layers. Take the top layer off, there's more to uncover underneath. Remove another, there's still more. You get the idea?

This first forgiveness point is very general. Forgive yourself for the choices you had to make. Over time, the deception we begin to see and feel is that there is no alternative to whatever is going on. Truthfully, sometimes there may not be. For example, in childhood, you usually can't just leave your home if that's where the abuse is present. You're not old enough, you don't have resources, and you really may have nowhere else to go. So doing what is necessary to survive is what you do. In adulthood, if the abuser has managed to move you away from everyone and everything you know to a place where you know no one and have very little or no resources, you also may not be able to go anywhere immediately.

And then, there's the trap of our minds. In my case, I had the ability and means to leave. I was stuck in a trauma bond and believed that I could not. In full honesty, it took a therapist to help me see that part clearly. I would teeter around it but never actually walk into the reality of it. When you are out of the danger that caused you to be in survival mode, you remain stuck in the mind trap of it all. You're clearly out but your mind tells you, you're still in.

Before we move any further, let's clear the air of a few things. God is not mad at you for the choices you made. He never left you. He was always with you, even though we might have wondered from time to time. I have come to believe and, in many cases, have seen the proof, that God wastes absolutely nothing. He uses everything for His glory. The plot of the enemy is to kill, steal, and destroy. There was a plan to do all of that to you one way or another. It may have been attempts of physical death, theft, and destruction, or it could have been mental and emotional, or a combination of them all. The trauma was designed to move you away from purpose and away from God. It was supposed to trap you to the point that you either decided to live life in whatever blah fashion it was or you decided to take your own, never realizing or actualizing who it was God made you to be. He stopped that plan. You are here today because He kept you. You are out of survival mode because now, He's ready to move you into healing and what's next for you. He's already forgiven you. It's your turn to forgive yourself.

I am going to pray for you and then give you some space to add on your own.

Father,

We come to You today to first thank You for creating ways for us to survive the snares of the enemy sent through trauma. We are grateful for survival mode. And although we may be hurting, confused, and cloudy, we thank You and already count it done that You will be with us through it all. Lord, help us to forgive ourselves for the situations we felt we had no control over. Help us to forgive ourselves for remaining in survival mode longer than You intended for us to be there. We thank You for forgiving us and believe that with Your help and guidance, we will forgive ourselves and help others to forgive themselves as well. We give You thanks, praise, honor, and glory.

In Jesus' name, Amen

Reflection: *Continue the prayer and/or reflect on what you've learned about yourself in this chapter and jot down things that come to mind that you need to forgive yourself for. It's ok if it's not in detail. It's also ok if you can't think of anything specific and just stick with the general declaration.*

_____

_____

_____

_____

_____

_____

_____

_____

_____

_____

_____

_____

_____

_____

_____

CHAPTER 5
Pray it Through

One of the things that I can now look back on and admit is that, had I kept a steady prayer life, I could have possibly avoided a lot of what I went through. And I don't mean just saying grace over food, asking for protection while driving, and prayers for sleep but like spending time daily talking with the Lord. I didn't do that enough. On occasion, I did, but clearly not enough. In fact, I don't think my consistent prayer life started until I wholeheartedly wanted to get out of the relationship.

(Remember, God wastes nothing! He'll use anything to bring you back to Him!)

I can share this now, and I don't believe I've said much about it in anything else that I've written or spoken. But the actual decision I made to get married was all a part of me being in survival mode and being trauma bonded. I got married in May of 2018, but unknown to most is that a few short months earlier, in January and definitely by February, I'd decided to be done with the whole thing and move on with life. How all of that came to change I discuss in *I Married Him Now What - A Saved Girl's Guide to Surviving Abusive Marriage*, but short version, I was in the narcissistic abuse cycle and didn't know it. A major part of my rationale was that getting married would fix, change, and do something positive with the current state of the relationship. Even though at the time, I was developing a prayer life, it was still fresh and new. I was still working on renewing my mind. (I also now know that mind renewal is a daily thing!)

Referring back to our Bible story, in the midst of the storm the Apostle Paul continued to pray and ask for guidance, even when he knew things weren't going to go well. It's the same for us in survival mode. As long as we are in that frame of mind, our decision-making is going to be slightly poor and highly questionable. And I know these are hard pills to swallow but in order to begin to come out of this thing and stay out, we have to be vigilant about facing the realities, the actual ones, not the perceived ones.

Normally our prayers go something like, "Dear Lord … insert pleasantries … insert requests … insert Thank You in advance, in Jesus' name, Amen." Then we open our eyes and go on about the rest of our days/nights. We get up too quickly. The problem isn't that we don't pray, the problem is really that we don't wait for answers. Prayer is supposed to be a method of two-way communication. We talk to God, and then when we're done, He talks back to us. Having realized that, we can collectively do a better job of waiting to hear from God before making moves. We are working on forgiving ourselves. We forgive ourselves for not having a strong prayer life or a prayer life at all. We forgive ourselves for the choices we made where we jumped the gun and didn't wait for the clarity of an answer before moving. We also repent, for the times when we didn't pray at all but just moved.

Use the space provided to do two things. First, if you don't already have one, develop a prayer schedule for yourself. Include the day of the week, the block of time, and the location. For example, in the beginning, part of my prayer schedule was my daily drive to work in the morning. Instead of turning on the radio, I would have a conversation with God and I would do the same thing coming home in the afternoon. If you have a prayer schedule already, evaluate it. Are you keeping to it? Do you need to make changes to it, such as pray longer, change your location, or the time of day? Jot down your schedule, and remember putting things in writing helps you to remember them.

The second thing I would like for you to do is to write your thoughts, feelings, and reflections about your past prayer time. Write down what you do well and what you would change. If you can think of any, set yourself prayer time goals. In coming out of survival mode, you have to use all of your armor and tools. Prayer is a weapon. We're going to learn how to accurately use it. You can even think of things you'd like to know about prayer and research them if you're able. I don't claim to be a prayer expert but if you have questions, you can always contact me and we'll talk about it.

Reflection: Write down your prayer schedule and anything else you want to note about developing/re-developing your prayer life.

_____

_____

_____

_____

_____

_____

_____

_____

_____

_____

_____

_____

_____

_____

_____

_____

I FORGIVE ME

_____

_____

_____

_____

_____

_____

_____

_____

_____

_____

_____

_____

_____

_____

_____

_____

_____

_____

TAKHIA GAITHER

CHAPTER 6
Movement May Not Mean You're Out

This one is "a toughy!" For me, I kind of didn't know that it was a thing until I'd actually done it. Short of a blaring, flashing, neon sign, there was nothing that could have told me I was still in survival mode when I went down the aisle. For starters, I didn't even know that's where I was until after the fact. As you read through this book and do the activities, you may now have similar revelations about your situation. You went into something believing you were "good," only to find out that in hindsight, not so much.

This one is very similar to jumping the gun after prayer. It could very well be the same. For me, I'd started doing a lot of inner healing work and deliverance. I was building the prayer life from the last step. It was becoming more consistent and I was learning to get answers but it was still in progress. I'd started reading the Bible daily, studying, and reflecting. That's how I started with the daily, (now mostly daily), IG encouragement posts. I had scriptures and reflections on index cards in my desk drawer and decided to start sharing them. I'd participated in a deliverance event and felt the chains breaking and all that good stuff. The reality is that while I was definitely moving in a positive direction, I was far from done. In fact, at the time, I was probably halfway through that particular process. Had I pushed the wedding back a few months to actually finish the course, there may not have been a wedding. That story is in a different book, back to survival and forgiveness for this one.

These things are repetitive and ongoing. Even in writing this book, there are still things coming up for me that I have to stop, think about, and forgive myself for. You will probably go through these steps more than one time. It's ok to do so and in fact, you should. Deliverance is not a one-time event. It requires effort to stay delivered. In going back to number 1, part of understanding that you are in or have been in survival mode is understanding how you got there, not just the specific circumstances, but especially in adulthood, the things you did to remain there. When we stay it's like putting a regular-size band-aid on a wound that needs stitches. It's only poorly and minimally covering or healing anything. It may have been sufficient enough for then, but it's not meant to continue on the journey to healing. I'm going to pray and then we'll talk a little more about the activity and reflection for this section.

Father in the name of Jesus,

We come today to thank You for Your love, guidance, and mercy as we have travailed through life in survival mode. Lord, we know that if it had not been for Your covering and protection, we would have been consumed by the pressures of the situations we faced. We thank You for keeping us safe, especially in the times when we moved before You. As we move through these activities, show us ourselves and give us the grace and peace to be able to take the sight. Help us as we endeavor to grow more and become closer to you. When things arise, remind us that You are with us and that in You we have everything we need to overcome this and any other situation or challenge. We give You all thanks, praise, honor, and glory.

In Jesus' name, Amen

This exercise is going to require you to quiet yourself and your surroundings. It's called prophetic journaling. You do not have to be a prophet to do it. You just have to want to hear God and have your ears open to what He has to say. For each question/prompt you will set a timer for 3-5 minutes. Before you start, pray for your ears, eyes, and heart to be open to what the Lord has to say. You can do it in silence, or you can choose to have music behind you. The Resources QR code will have a link to some of my favorite journaling and writing music. Set the timer before you ask the question. Start the music, ask the question, start the timer, and write what you hear or see. Listen for the still small voice. Once you have your instructions, follow them.

Question 1 - *Father God, am I still in Survival Mode? If not, what do You want me to know about my current mental state regarding my situation?*

_____

_____

_____

_____

_____

_____

_____

_____

_____

_____

_____

_____

_____

_____

_____

_____

_____

_____

_____

_____

_____

_____

_____

_____

_____

_____

_____

_____

_____

_____

_____

_____

_____

Question 2 - *Lord, what should I do next?*

_____

_____

_____

_____

_____

_____

_____

_____

_____

_____

_____

_____

_____

_____

_____

TAKHIA GAITHER

Chapter 7
Don't Be Afraid to Throw Away Things

About a year before the pandemic, the counselor I was seeing gave me a piece of advice that I carry with me until this day and I share it whenever I feel it's appropriate to do so. In coming out of survival mode it's definitely appropriate to do so, especially if fawning is one of your top two. We were talking about why I didn't feel like I could leave a situation even though I completely had the financial means, resources, and enough ingenuity to do so. As I started rattling off this list of "reasons," she stopped me and said, "But is that really something you have control over? Like is that your direct problem to deal with?" It stopped me in my tracks and as I thought about it, the answer to both questions was no. She said, "When you evaluate situations and the bottom line is not something you have control over, your next move is to hand people their stuff back."

Poof, mind blown! For years, I'd been carrying things that had nothing to do with me. And those things were also usually the things that sent me into fight mode because I obviously cared way more about the situation than its owner. Over the course of years, I'd unknowingly begun to bear the burden of someone else's poor decisions, choices, habits, and lack of abilities. Even in trying to teach or show that individual how to do things differently, I would become frustrated because they refused to learn. As a teacher, nothing irks my soul more than someone who has access to education but refuses to take it. It is at the absolute top of the list of things that grinds my gears. However, with my students, I quickly learned that I was not going to spoon-feed them anything because in doing that, I would enable them from becoming responsible adults and I didn't want that on me. In my personal life though, I could not seem to apply that same thing, mostly because I was under the impression that those choices or whatever somehow impacted me. Since I didn't want the backlash of their foolishness, I would end up just taking on whatever it was to get it done or to shut them up because I didn't want to hear the noise of it.

All of that to say to you today, "Hand people their stuff back." It's ok to throw away things that don't belong to you. As you begin to declutter your mind, heart, and even your physical space, forgive yourself for holding on to things that did not serve you well. It's ok if that includes the relationships with whoever. I would venture to say, that we didn't go into these relationships, be they familial or romantic, with ill intentions. We wanted to provide love, care, and support to those we had connections with. That is completely normal and it is what we were created to do as people. However, when we see things that become burdensome for no real reason that we can tell, it's time to assess the situation. It's hard to see things when you're knee-deep in them. This is where what I like to call your "Circle of Safety" comes into play. The "Circle of Safety" is about 3-5 people who can be your safe spaces. They are the people you can talk to without judgment. They support you but also do what they can and what is necessary to help guide you in ways that are useful and non-damaging. They may be friends, relatives, counselors, pastors, or whomever you decide. Over time my circle has changed but there are a few core people who haven't changed. Even when I didn't want to hear their opinions regarding my relationship, I knew and trusted they would tell the honest truth about it. (Funny enough story now, but my friends actually came to the wedding to object. They didn't because they couldn't hear the preacher when he said that part.)

If you are coming out of an abusive romantic relationship, it is very possible that the friends you once had are now ostracized or you're just not near them. It is paramount to your healing to find a community. Oddly enough, when I felt like my circle didn't really understand, I turned to Facebook groups. Just did a random search one day. I was looking for support group-type settings and I found a few groups that were really informational and inspirational. I wouldn't call those people my friends, but when I needed to bounce off ideas or discuss things that I was seeing but being gaslit about, they were helpful. My caution to you is that these groups can become emotionally overwhelming very quickly. Although initially they were helpful, over time, scrolling through posts daily became a task that I had to throw away. Occasionally, I visit a few of them to provide support to others, just like someone showed support to me. You don't have to tell them all your business, and sometimes misery does love company so be prayerful about what you choose to say and whom you chose to listen to if you decide to take that route. You want people who will encourage you and help you clear your mind, not add more stress to it.

For the first activity, find a loose sheet of paper, (don't mess up a good journal by ripping out pages!). Make a list of things that you are holding on to that don't belong to you. If you believe you're not holding anything, pray into it. When you finish your list, go through each thing and say "I forgive myself for holding on to _____. I release it." You are making declarations and letting go of the trash. When you've finished the list destroy the paper to symbolize that you are no longer emotionally, mentally, or physically holding on to any of those things.

The second activity might take a little longer. I'm still in this phase but it's definitely becoming easier, day by day. Begin to purge your home and your belongings of things that don't belong to you. If they left it, get rid of it. I even went so far as to get rid of gifts and cards that came from my ex. I chucked photos and threw away paperwork, id cards, and clothes - whatever it was, if it didn't belong to me or my children, it went out. It becomes too heavy to keep carrying these things, you'll sink. Sinking will send you right back into

survival mode. Just like they did in the story, toss it overboard.

TAKHIA GAITHER

CHAPTER 8
LIVE!

" The thief comes only to steal and kill and destroy; I have come that they may have life, and have it to the full," John 10:10. I could really end the chapter, the book, this whole discussion right here!

Listen, Beloved, God has not kept us here to not live life abundantly! We have a purpose, we have things to do, and we have to dreams to fulfill. There's so much more for us than staying in this place of mundane nothingness. That's not what we're here for. Forgive yourself for not living, for not seeing then what you know now, for letting whatever keep you stagnant and not moving.

Survival mode kicked in to stop the trap set by the enemy from killing you. Once death was off the table, it kept on going to steal your joy, your resolve, and your resilience and set you on a path to destroy everything about you until you almost didn't recognize yourself. I'm very passionate about this part because I know for a fact that this is what happened to me. I saw how the story was supposed to end and I heard God say, "Not so. You will live and not die." I don't take it lightly or for granted that I'm still here, sane, and have been empowered and emboldened to help others.

I want to encourage you to live. Live for yourself. If you're a mother or a person who's responsible for others in some capacity, live for those you love. They won't be better without you. They need you. You need you! The Lord has need of you. You have yet to see the best of your life. There will be beauty for these ashes.

For the activity in this section, we're going to work on setting some goals. I'm going to create space for one goal here, but if you're the ambitious type, feel free to set more. If you've never set a goal before or successfully completed one, then we're going to take this slow and just go with one for now. Many of us set goals for lots of things, to get degrees, specific types of jobs, to write books, or start businesses. Even in survival mode, you may have thought of goals and had good intentions of pursuing them but just didn't. There was never enough time and what you wanted to do or needed to do seemed to get taken over by something else.

One of the things that unnerved me a bit when I first realized that I was coming out of survival mode was the amount of "free" time I actually had. I was married for 4 years and in a situationship with him for somewhere around 10 years before that, probably longer. The last time I remembered having completely free time to just do whatever I wanted to do whenever I wanted to do it was somewhere around 2009. For a while, my goal was to do nothing and enjoy it. I almost enjoyed it a little too much, lol. Learning to create SMART goals for my business snapped me back into reality and productivity.

SMART is an acronym. It stands for Specific, Measurable, Achievable, Relevant, and Time-bound, (or time-specific as I like to say). It's easy to set empty goals and just run off a list of things you want to accomplish, but the reason why we generally don't accomplish them is that we don't take the time to properly map them out. As I'm explaining each section, I'm going to use my writing of this book as an example. I'm also going to include some other resources to help with writing your goals, including some templates you can print and hang up after you've completed them. You may want to do this part using a pencil with a good eraser! You'll want to be able to make changes.

Goal Step	Definition	Example
S **Specific**	Make your goal as specific and narrow as possible. For a huge goal, break it down into steps, and turn each step into a goal. It's even ok to jot down your large goal, and then list out the pieces.	Write a book about forgiveness in survival mode.
M **Measurable**	Set points that you will be able to check off to say you're moving towards completing the goal.	A completed book on Amazon and other vendors in print, eBook, and possibly audio format.
A **Achievable/ Attainable**	Make sure your goal is something that you can actually do. At this point, I like to think about what I need to make it happen and put down some action steps.	- Create a writing plan around the topic. - Research survival mode - Jot down a tentative outline/notes - Write the rough draft (by hand or just start typing)

		- Self-edit, get proofreading, do the final formatting - Submit for self-publishing companies
R **Relevant**	What is your why for achieving this goal? How is it relevant to your life or business or whatever your reason is for having it?	This book is part of what I now see as a series. They're not order specific, but they are the books that chronicle my journey, growth, and lessons through abuse, separation, divorce, and trauma. Large goal for the year - to publish 10 books of my own by the end of the year.
T **Time Bound (Specific)**	Set a date to have your goal completed. You may also want to include dates with each of the steps you outlined in the Attainable/Achievable section.	December/January - Begin planning and research February - Write the book! March - Editing, proofing,

		formatting, publishing

If this is the first time you've done an activity like this, it might seem a little overwhelming. It's ok. Break the task into smaller pieces. Don't feel like you have to know all the things at one time. Additionally, understand that things will change. The thing with goals is that usually, you don't know what's involved to make them happen until you start doing it. The idea is to keep moving forward, in spite of the changes and challenges. You have to live. It requires steps. You will have to do the work and participate in your own healing. Check out the resources for a blank editable version of the chart above so that you can begin to set your goals and create a path to completion.

TAKHIA GAITHER

CHAPTER 9
Believe You Are an Overcomer

I t's often said, "Nothing changes until you do." I partially agree with that. Nothing changes until your *mindset* changes. When you change your perspective, you will begin to create a different outcome. Forgive yourself for doubting yourself.

Up to this point, we've done so much. We've come to grips with some really hard topics and some really big things. We've put language to this hum-drum existence we've been going through. We've identified triggers, decided to reset, grown in prayer, and so much more. Think back to when you first started with this book. We've developed some history here. I'm excited for you! You are an overcomer! You've got this and God's got you.

Every once in a while, you'll have to tell the enemy to kick rocks in the rain or just rebuke the negativity and the lies. Satan is the father of lies, for all I care, he can beat it like Michael Jackson, I don't have time for his foolishness. Understanding and knowing that you can overcome does not negate your emotions or feelings about anything you're going through or have gone through. It is your decision to be honest with yourself and others if need be, about how you're feeling and your declaration to keep going.

One of my favorite scriptures is Philippians 4:8, "Finally, brothers and sisters, whatever is true, whatever is noble, whatever is right, whatever is pure, whatever is lovely, whatever is admirable—if anything is excellent or praiseworthy—think about such things." When things don't look the way I think they should or to be honest, they're absolutely horrible, this scripture is how I shift my thought patterns. I had to learn to counteract every negative thought with the word of God. To do that I had to build my scripture memory bank.

We're going to do a few things here - take it back to Sunday School with memory verses, create some devotional pieces, and learn to encourage ourselves. We can actually accomplish all three tasks with one activity. As I mentioned earlier, I wrote encouragement pieces on index cards before I started posting them to social media. They were my reminders. On difficult days, I would flip through the ring of cards, read them, and then read the reflections, sometimes I'd even add more to what I'd written previously. In the space provided here, make a list of your 10 favorite scriptures or if you don't have 10 favorites, use 10 scriptures for encouragement, (you can type the topic into Google and pick out verses that stand out to you). Next, you'll need index cards, a single-hole puncher, and a binder ring, (you can get all of these things from your local dollar store). On the front of the index card, write out the scripture - the words of the verse, the book, the chapter, the verse, and which Bible translation you are using. On the back, write a short note about what it says to you. It may be sentences or just a few words, but it's your thoughts about that verse. Keep them someplace that you can refer to them often. If you find that you're struggling with the back of the index card, just write the verses for now. As you revisit your scriptures, inspiration or enlightenment will come.

You will do this for 10 days, but feel free to continue past the initial 10. This activity became part of my daily devotional prayer time that we established way back in the prayer chapter. Remember, writing builds memory. The road to becoming, being, and remaining an overcomer is full of doubts, hurdles, and just things. The way to combat these things is to speak the word to and over the situations. Immediately, it may not change what you see or what's going on, but what it will do is change how you see or react to the situation. I've included space for you to create your initial list.

Reflection: *List your 10 favorite encouraging scriptures and/or 10 scriptures to begin your index card memory book.*

_____

_____

_____

_____

_____

_____

_____

_____

_____

_____

_____

_____

_____

_____

_____

_____

TAKHIA GAITHER

CHAPTER 10
Assess the Damages and Move On

Collateral damage is a term originally used to describe incidents in a war where more was lost than the soldiers of the opposing side or things lost outside of the initial target. I've come to use it to describe various events in my personal life, which sometimes felt like a war zone. Despite my best efforts to solely take the impact of the craziness that was my life, there was definitely collateral damage. That's not always a good feeling but it must be acknowledged.

Sleep, peace, money, residences, vehicles, almost jobs, opportunities, and sleep, (because it's worth saying twice) … Just a few of the things that were lost during survival mode. Some of them were casualties. For instance, I was in a car accident that totaled the vehicle. Indirectly, it had nothing to do with survival mode, however, in thinking back to the circumstances of life during that time, it did. I got into the accident after having picked my son up from school because it had become a necessity that I get him because his father would be too tired to pick him up. To alleviate getting phone calls saying that no one had come to get him from school, I would leave work, nearly fly from where I was working to the neighborhood where I lived and pick him up. You see, related but not related, right?

In reflecting on the totality of the relationship from start to finish, there were several of these types of losses. When you start reviewing or thinking about those things, it can be really depressing, to be honest. It just looks like loss and devastation. Evaluating the losses is what led me to have a "silver lining" outlook on just about everything. Back to Philippians 4:8, yes I'm facing a loss but in the loss what is the thing that is good, true, and holy? You may not get to the silver lining part, but you will develop your own way to assess and evaluate your situations in ways that are useful, helpful, and healthy.

Today, we're going to find some silver linings. Back to the example of my vehicle being totaled. The silver lining was that neither myself nor my child was injured, I had money left over from the payoff to go towards a new vehicle, and the vehicle that was lost was beginning to have problems so I actually needed a new one anyway. Were these all things that I was able to see right away? Not the first day and definitely not as I was sitting in the ER to make sure I was ok and that child #2 was ok in the womb.

On the pages that follow you'll see a t-chart. On one side you're going to list the loss, on the other side directly across you're going to write out the silver lining. If you can't think of anything at the time, it's ok, leave some space and come back to it. Your silver linings don't have to be profound or lengthy. They don't need to be these elaborate statements. My example is my thought process through things, yours's will be different. If you need help finding the silver lining, my inbox is always open. Given enough time, I can always find one.

THE LOSSES | ## THE SILVER LININGS

TAKHIA GAITHER

84

CHAPTER 11

I'm Letting It Go

Well, you've made it! Where you ask?

To the end of the book, to past where you were at the beginning of it, perhaps completely out of survival mode, you've made it to the day and time that you are reading this and that is an accomplishment. I'm clapping for your win!

This is a tough thing to walk through. And trust me, although I'm sitting here writing the book, I'm still walking through it. It's an ongoing process. You didn't get in this predicament overnight; you're not coming out overnight either. In this case, I won't say time will heal your wounds, but I will say, in time, your wounds will heal. That's important for you to remember that. Things will get better in time.

Our final activity is the release. It's such a powerful activity. You'll need a permanent marker and a balloon, preferably a light-colored one so you can see what you write. You may also want to do this activity with friends or a support group. I did it at a women's retreat with my church. Blow up the balloon and tie it. On the balloon, begin to write the things you need to forgive yourself for doing while you were in survival mode. It's ok if you use more than one balloon. If you need a little music to set the mood as you do this, be sure to check out the I Forgive Me Playlist on the resources. This doesn't have to be super long; the length of a song-playing should give you enough time to write out what you need to. You can use words, phrases, or whole sentences if you choose.

When you're done writing tie a string to the balloons and take them outside. Once you're outside, play James Fortune's I Forgive Me. Let the verses minister to you for a bit. At about the halfway mark of the song, around two minutes and forty seconds (2:40), let the balloons go. As you watch the balloons fly away into the great beyond, take some time to breathe in the goodness and love of God at that moment. Let Him love on you as you release things that have been holding you for far too long. You may cry, you may feel an overwhelming sense of relief, you may not know exactly what you're feeling right then, or you may feel a combination. Whatever you feel, let them come. It's ok to feel them all. Believe that it is gone, God has forgiven you. Your future is bright. You have a future. The only person that can stop you is you. Today you are declaring that you're done stopping you. It's time for you to forgive you.

Reflection: Now that you've released it all, how do you feel?

_____

_____

_____

_____

_____

_____

_____

_____

_____

_____

_____

_____

_____

_____

_____

_____

_____

_____

_____
_____
_____
_____
_____
_____
_____
_____
_____
_____
_____
_____
_____
_____
_____
_____
_____

CLOSING PRAYER

Father God,

As we've come to the end of this workbook, we give You thanks for forgiving us and loving us through the times we didn't know how to forgive ourselves. I pray that the words and activities in these pages have led the reader to a deeper relationship with You and to an understanding of the importance of forgiving themselves. Please remind them that they have a future, and they don't have to stay in this stagnant place. Father if they've moved from this place, continue to walk with them as move towards living life more abundantly. Let us walk in the John 10:10 life. I pray for their hearts, minds, and all that they put their hands to. I pray that they find their purpose ordained by You and begin to walk boldly in it. I rebuke any evil or negative thought that may try to consume them and convince them that where they are is where they will always be. Lord, we shut the mouth of the enemy and declare that we will be the people You've called us to be and will be a light and example to others of Your grace, mercy, and love that they may come to know You in the pardoning of their sins. Lord, let nothing that we've said or done be in vain and that it all be used to the glory and honor of You. We give You all thanks and praise for all You've done and all that You will do. We love You. We thank You.

In Jesus' name, Amen.

RESOURCES

Scan the QR code to be taken to the I Forgive Me Resources page where you'll find links to the worksheets, blank journal pages, books for further reading, and the special playlists I've created just for you as you are on your self-forgiveness journey. I pray that it all encourages and aids you. God bless!

NOTES

NOTES

NOTES

NOTES

NOTES

ABOUT THE AUTHOR

Takhia Gaither decided during the pandemic that there would be no more hiding! To date she has co-authored over 10 anthologies, 3 of which were Amazon Bestsellers in multiple categories, written and created a Bible Study Workbook – *Be the Overcomer*, written for various online publications, created lined inspirational journals, both yearly and financial planners, and currently maintains two blogs. In the fall of 2022, she launched the Redefining Thoughts Podcast and YouTube shows. Her portfolio continues to grow with new book projects to be unveiled beginning in the spring of 2023, in addition to becoming an international TEDx speaker and curriculum writer and moving into traveling as a speaker, teacher, and coach.

Takhia is a mother, retired educator, author, editor, and certified Christian Confidence and Mental Health Coach, with a specialization in trauma-informed coaching to be completed summer of 2023. Writing has always been a hobby, so in 2018 she began her blog, *Takhia the Teacher,* and began writing as a volunteer for the online publication *Godly Today.* She started The Ready Write-Her editing, copywriting, and formatting company in 2019 as a profitable hobby. With the release of her first anthology, *She Changed Her Narrative,* she also became a published editor. Throughout the process of writing, she received countless confirmations that her years of teaching were moving her from public school to the classroom of life. In addition to editing, she is also a writing coach for new authors who seek training and accountability as they prepare their stories for the world to see. Follow her on the web and on social media:

Web – thereadywrite-her.com

Blogs – tsgsgroup.com/redefiningyou
          takhiatheteacher.wixsite.com/ttheteach

Facebook, Instagram & Pinterest – takhiatheteacher

YouTube – bit.ly/redefiningthoughts
             bit.ly/TakhiaTheTeacher

E-Mail – thereadywrite-her@tsgsgroup.com